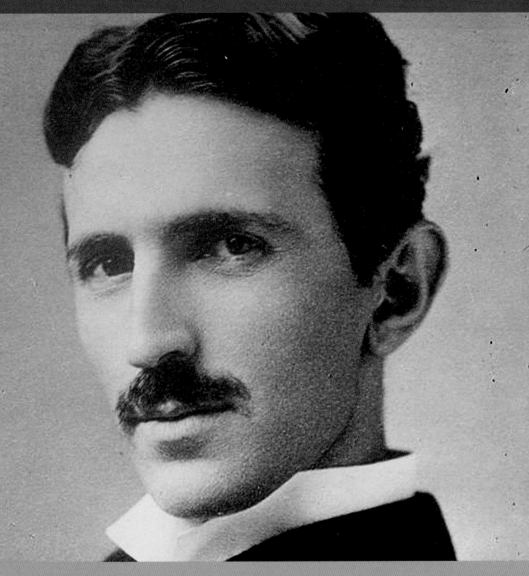

12 IMMIGRANTS WHO MADE
AMERICAN
SCIENCE GREAT

by Tristan Poehlmann

www.12StoryLibrary.com

12-Story Library is an imprint of Bookstaves.

Photographs ©: Library of Congress, cover, 1; PD, 4; Wellcome Collection/CC 4.0, 5; Time, Inc. UPI Photo Service/Newscom, 6; Al. Aumuller/Library of Congress, 7; Science History Images/Alamy Stock Photo, 8; Smithsonian Institution Archives/PD, 9; PD, 9; Bettmann/Getty Images, 10; NASA/UMass/D.Wang et al., 11; Gjon Mili/The LIFE Picture Collection/Getty Images, 12; Science Service (Smithsonian Institution)/CC, 13; ZUMA Press, Inc./Alamy Stock Photo, 14; NASA, 15; PD, 16; NASA/JPL-Caltech/MSSS, 17; Janwikifoto/CC3.0, 18; NASA's Earth Observatory, 19; PD, 20; ilikestudio/Shutterstock.com, 21; Holger Motzkau/CC3.0, 22; vrx/Shutterstock.com, 23; US Department of Energy National Laboratory/University of California, 24; NASA, 25; Alchetron/CC3.0, 26; Fermilab, Reidar Hahn/PD, 27; Justinvasel/CC4.0, 27; Smithsonian Institution/CC, 28; Rodarenas/CC4.0, 29

ISBN
978-1-63235-576-8 (hardcover)
978-1-63235-630-7 (paperback)
978-1-63235-691-8 (ebook)

Library of Congress Control Number: 2018937978

Printed in the United States of America
Mankato, MN
July 2018

About the Cover
Nicola Tesla in 1890.

Access free, up-to-date content on this topic plus a full digital version of this book. Scan the QR code on page 31 or use your school's login at 12StoryLibrary.com.

Table of Contents

1

Nikola Tesla Lights Up the World

The world runs on electricity because of Nikola Tesla. He invented the power system we use today. He also thought up wireless communication.

Tesla was born in 1856. He lived in the mountains of what is now Croatia. Tesla's family was Serbian. His father was a priest in the Serbian Orthodox Church. His mother invented clever household tools.

Tesla studied math and physics in school. He learned engineering. In 1884, he immigrated to the United States. He began working for Thomas Edison. But Tesla disagreed with Edison's ideas. Edison used direct current (DC) electricity. Tesla had an idea he believed would be more efficient.

In 1887, Tesla started his own company. He developed a system to generate alternating current (AC) electricity. In 1893, Tesla demonstrated his system at the Chicago World's Fair. The crowd was impressed. The invention brought him money and respect. Tesla was hired to design a new power plant. It would generate power from

4

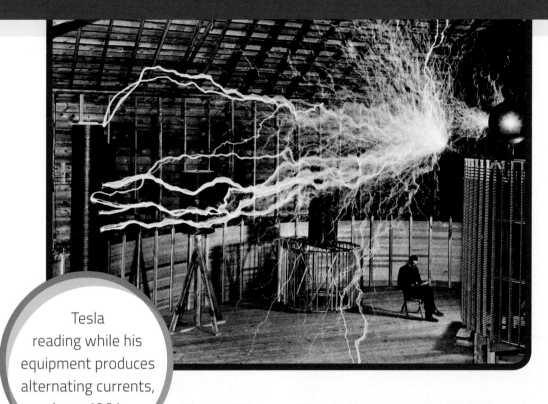

Tesla reading while his equipment produces alternating currents, June, 1901.

Niagara Falls. He designed a system that worked perfectly. It produced enough electricity to light New York City.

Tesla's ideas were ahead of his time. He believed the world could be connected wirelessly. He predicted many things about the future.

THE MAD SCIENTIST

People often found Tesla's habits odd. His meals had to be boiled. He washed his hands constantly. He was very afraid of germs. But he loved to feed the pigeons in New York City parks. He even took hurt pigeons home. He nursed them back to health.

112
Number of US patents held by Nikola Tesla.

- Tesla emigrated from Croatia in 1884 for a job.
- He was an electrical engineer and inventor.
- The power system he developed is still used today.

Albert Einstein Explains Space and Time

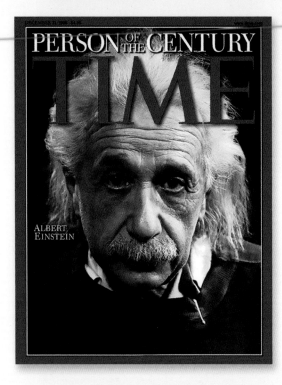

In 1999, *TIME* magazine named Albert Einstein Person of the Century. Einstein was a scientist whose ideas stunned the world. He changed how we think about the universe.

Einstein was born in Germany in 1879. His family was Jewish. Einstein's father wanted him to study electrical engineering. Einstein did not like school, but he was very curious. He taught himself math and physics. He passed his university exams despite not going to class.

In 1905, Einstein changed physics forever. He published a series of new ideas. One was the math equation $E = mc^2$. It explained how matter is turned into energy. He also published his theory of special relativity. The theory came from Einstein's thought experiments.

Einstein liked to picture his ideas in his mind. He could figure out whether or not they were right. One thought experiment was about light speed. He pictured traveling on a wave of light. He realized something. At light speed, time passes at a different rate. Einstein discovered that space and time depend on point of view. In 1921, he won the Nobel Prize in Physics.

Einstein's thought experiments were scientific tools. He was able to imagine how light would travel through space. How would you prepare for your own thought experiment?

In 1933, Adolf Hitler banned Jewish professors from teaching. Einstein lost his job. He immigrated to the United States to continue his work. Einstein's influence helped physics grow in America.

4

Number of physics papers Albert Einstein published in 1905.

- Einstein emigrated from Germany in 1933 to escape discrimination.
- He was a physicist who helped create modern physics.
- He developed the theory of relativity and the math equation $E = mc^2$

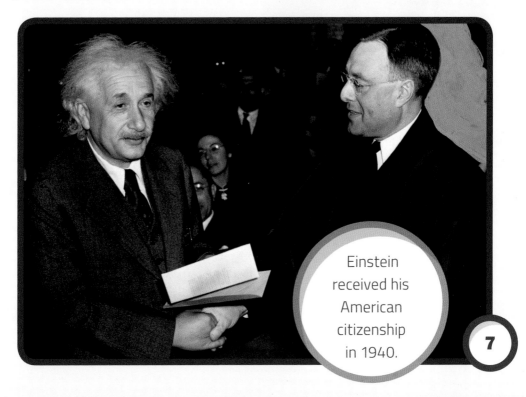

Einstein received his American citizenship in 1940.

3

Maria Goeppert-Mayer Maps the Atomic Nucleus

In 1963, a woman won the Nobel Prize in Physics. She was the second woman to win. Her work was groundbreaking. She explained how atoms worked inside.

Maria Goeppert was born in 1906. Her family lived in a part of Germany that today is Poland. They were an educated family. Goeppert's father trained medical doctors. He encouraged his daughter to study science. She learned math and physics. In 1930, Goeppert earned the highest degree in physics. She married an American chemist named Joseph Edward Mayer. She immigrated to the United States with him.

Goeppert-Mayer's husband became a professor. The couple worked at several universities. She worked as an unpaid assistant researcher. Her work was important, however. She began to study the structure of atoms. Little was known about the nucleus inside an atom. Goeppert-Mayer spent years studying the nucleus.

In 1949, Goeppert-Mayer discovered how the nucleus worked. She

developed a mathematical model of it. The model explained the structure of the nucleus. It also explained why some atoms are more stable than others. Stable atoms are less radioactive.

Goeppert-Mayer's work helped scientists understand radioactivity. In 1955, she published a book about her discovery. Her book is titled *Elementary Theory of Nuclear Shell Structure*. In 1960, she finally became a paid university professor. Three years later, she won the Nobel Prize.

15
Years of research Maria Goeppert-Mayer did as a volunteer.

- Goeppert-Mayer emigrated from Germany in 1930 to be with family.
- She was a physicist who discovered how the atomic nucleus works.
- Her mathematical model explained why some atoms are radioactive.

Subrahmanyan Chandrasekhar Discovers Black Holes

Chandrasekhar with reporters on October 19, 1983, the day he won the Nobel Prize in Physics.

In Britain, Chandrasekhar studied astrophysics. He developed a theory about the life cycle of stars. He discovered there was a limit to the mass of a star. A star reaching that limit would collapse. But other scientists did not accept this theory. They did not believe stars could die violently. Chandrasekhar believed his theory was correct. He had proved it mathematically. But he decided to move on.

The universe is full of stars. But stars do not live forever. Subrahmanyan Chandrasekhar was the first scientist to learn how they die.

Chandrasekhar was born in 1910. His family lived in India. His father worked for the British government. His uncle was a physicist. Chandrasekhar learned math and science by reading books. He won a scholarship to attend Cambridge University.

In 1937, he became a professor at the University of Chicago. He worked in many areas of astrophysics. Over time, the idea of stars collapsing was accepted. Chandrasekhar's theory was proved right. In the 1960s, scientists began to call collapsed stars black holes. Chandrasekhar returned to work on the idea. He published *The Mathematical Theory of Black Holes* in 1983.

X-RAY CLOSE-UP

A magnified image of a black hole in the Milky Way galaxy, taken by the Hubble Space Telescope.

30

Years that passed before Subrahmanyan Chandrasekhar's star collapse theory was accepted.

- Chandrasekhar emigrated from India in 1937 for a job.
- He was an astrophysicist who discovered black holes.
- His work proved that a star's life cycle ends with its collapse.

Chandrasekhar's early work was ahead of its time. He discovered that dying stars collapse into black holes. He built the foundation for the theory of black holes. In 1983, he won the Nobel Prize in Physics.

Oxford Classic Texts
IN THE PHYSICAL SCIENCES

The Mathematical Theory of Black Holes

S. Chandrasekhar

Chien-Shiung Wu Breaks a Law of Physics

She was often called the First Lady of Physics, but she never won a Nobel Prize. Her name was Chien-Shiung Wu. Her most famous experiment changed modern physics.

Wu was born in 1912. She grew up in a small town in China. Her father wanted her to be educated. He started a girls' school in their town. Wu learned science by reading books. In college, she studied physics. In 1936, she immigrated to the United States. She wanted to go to graduate school.

Wu studied at the University of California, Berkeley. She became an expert in nuclear physics. She knew how to create energy by splitting the nucleus inside an atom. She became a researcher at Columbia University. During World War II, Wu did research for the Manhattan Project. Its goal was to develop a bomb that used nuclear energy.

After the war, Wu did experiments on radioactivity. Her work was on

6

Months it took Chien-Shiung Wu to plan her famous experiment.

- Wu emigrated from China in 1936 for school.
- She was a physicist known as the First Lady of Physics.
- Her experimental work changed the laws of physics.

THINK ABOUT IT

Wu's research helped the United States develop nuclear technology. One result was the atomic bomb. How much should scientists think about the ways their research might be used?

the cutting edge of science. In 1957, she proved that a law of physics was wrong. The discovery was huge. It was on the front pages of newspapers. The scientists she worked with won a Nobel Prize. Wu did not.

Wu won many other awards, however. In 1975, she won the National Medal of Science. Wu's work changed science. She proved that the laws of nature can be broken.

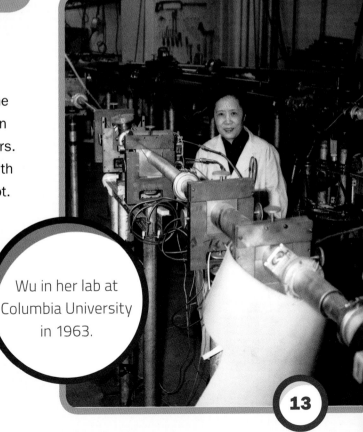

Wu in her lab at Columbia University in 1963.

Arno Allan Penzias Hears the Big Bang

The beginning of the universe is a mystery. But scientists have a good theory about it. Arno Allan Penzias helped prove that theory.

Penzias was born in Germany in 1933. His family was Jewish. The Nazi government abused Jews. Penzias left Germany when he was six. His parents put him on a train to Britain. He had to take care of his little brother. His parents arrived later. The family immigrated to the United States in 1940.

In New York, Penzias went to school. He wanted to be a scientist. First he learned chemistry. In college, he discovered physics. In graduate school, he studied radio waves in space. Penzias found a job at Bell Labs. They made antennae for satellite communication.

In 1964, Penzias started new research. He used a huge horn-shaped antenna. He tuned into radio waves from space. He planned to map them. But his antenna had a problem. Penzias kept hearing static noise. He tried everything to get rid of it. Then he realized what the static was. He had discovered cosmic radiation noise.

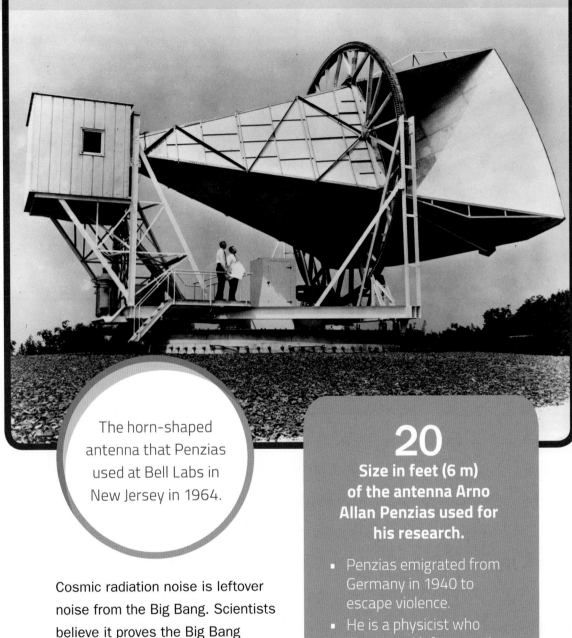

The horn-shaped antenna that Penzias used at Bell Labs in New Jersey in 1964.

20
Size in feet (6 m) of the antenna Arno Allan Penzias used for his research.

- Penzias emigrated from Germany in 1940 to escape violence.
- He is a physicist who discovered leftover noise from the Big Bang.
- His work helped prove the Big Bang theory of how the universe was formed.

Cosmic radiation noise is leftover noise from the Big Bang. Scientists believe it proves the Big Bang theory. The theory states that the universe was formed in an explosion. Penzias's work was very important. In 1978, he won the Nobel Prize in Physics.

7

Roseli Ocampo-Friedmann Grows Life from Rocks

Many scientists search for extraterrestrial life. Someday life on other planets may be discovered. But one

Ocampo-Friedmann, with husband Imre, holds an Antarctic rock sample from their research.

scientist has already collected the closest thing on Earth.

Roseli Ocampo was born in 1937 in the Philippines. She grew up in the city of Manila. In school, Ocampo studied plants. She finished college in 1958 with a degree in botany. She moved to Jerusalem and earned her master's degree.

In 1968, Ocampo immigrated to the United States. She finished her PhD in biology. She married another biologist, Imre Friedmann. Together they studied life in extreme environments. These are places on Earth where humans generally don't live. The two biologists traveled around the world. They found tiny life forms in hot and cold deserts. Ocampo-Friedmann collected samples. She grew them in her lab. This let her study the samples more closely.

The biologists visited Antarctica in the 1970s. They made an amazing

16

1,000

Number of samples Roseli Ocampo-Friedmann collected from extreme environments.

- Ocampo-Friedmann emigrated from the Philippines in 1968 for school.
- She was a biologist who studied life in harsh environments.
- She discovered life growing inside rocks in Antarctica.

LIFE ON MARS

The Search for Extraterrestrial Intelligence (SETI) Institute is a center for studying alien life. Ocampo-Friedmann worked there as a Mars Specialist. She understood how life forms survive in harsh climates. She helped explain how life could begin on planets like Mars. She knew where to look for life forms. Her work helps scientists today search for alien life.

discovery. Inside the rocks lived bacteria colonies. Ocampo-Friedmann developed a way to grow the bacteria. She figured out how the bacteria survived.

NASA was excited by their discovery. Perhaps rocks on Mars could hide life. Ocampo-Friedmann became interested in extraterrestrial life. NASA helped fund the biologists' research.

NASA's *Curiosity* rover drills for rock samples on Mars in 2015.

Mario Molina Saves the Ozone Layer

Scientists don't usually save the world. But Mario Molina won the Nobel Prize for something pretty close. He wanted to use science for good. And he did.

Molina was born in 1943. His family lived in Mexico. Growing up, he loved science. His bathroom was his laboratory. Molina's aunt was a chemist. She helped him with experiments. Molina studied chemistry in school. He went to college.

In 1968, Molina immigrated to the United States. He wanted a graduate degree in chemistry. He went to the University of California, Berkeley. Then he got a job as a researcher. He studied chemicals in the atmosphere. Earth's atmosphere traps many chemicals that we use. Molina wondered what effects this had. Did the chemicals harm Earth's atmosphere?

Molina studied chemicals called CFCs. They were very common. He discovered that CFCs are dangerous. They destroy ozone. The ozone layer is part of Earth's atmosphere. CFCs are damaging the atmosphere. In 1974, Molina published his research. Four years later, the United States banned CFCs.

The danger of CFCs was proved in 1983. Scientists found a hole in the ozone layer. Molina's discovery had been just in time. He won the Nobel Prize in Chemistry in 1995.

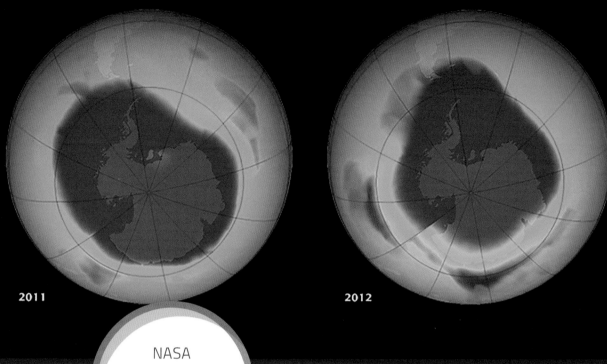

2011

2012

NASA image showing the recovery of the ozone layer.

40
Percent decrease in ozone recorded eight years after Mario Molina's discovery.

- Molina emigrated from Mexico in 1968 for school.
- He is a chemist who won the Nobel Prize.
- His research helped save Earth's ozone layer.

RETURN OF THE OZONE

There is a hole in the ozone layer above Antarctica. For many years, it was getting worse. But it will get better. In 2018, NASA announced that the ozone layer is recovering. The process is slow. NASA says the hole could be fixed by 2080. However, research also shows ozone changes above other continents. Scientists will keep studying the ozone layer.

Huda Akil Proves That Stress Changes the Brain

Vanderbilt Brain Institute

Human brains are complex. Scientists are still learning about them. Huda Akil was one of the first brain scientists to study feelings.

Akil was born in Syria in 1945. Her father was a psychologist. Akil became interested in how brains work. She wondered where feelings came from. She wanted to study the science of brains. Akil won a scholarship and went to college.

In 1968, Akil immigrated to the United States. She moved to Los Angeles for graduate school. There she studied how pain works in the brain. Her work showed that brains could block pain. They could release painkillers. Akil finished school. But she kept researching.

Akil discovered how the brain blocks pain. The painkillers are called endorphins. The brain releases them in response to stress. It is a survival method. The discovery of endorphins was very important. Scientists began to study stress. Akil's work changed the direction of brain science.

Today Akil researches how stress affects emotions. She studies the causes of depression and anxiety. She discovered links between stress and mental health. Her research shows that the brain is changed by its experiences. Brains are still mysterious. But Akil proved that feelings are part of biology.

2011

Year that Huda Akil was elected to the National Academy of Sciences.

- Akil emigrated from Syria in 1968 for school.
- She is a neurobiologist who studies emotions.
- She discovered that the brain can block pain.

TO FOLLOW A DREAM

Akil liked science when she was young. But the world centers of science were far from Syria. It seemed impossible to become a scientist. Then Akil read a book about Marie Curie. The physicist's story inspired her. If a girl from Poland could be a scientist, Akil thought she could, too. She decided to follow her dream.

happiness
sport
music balance balance medicine
feeling
food life care
relax
health endorphins happy
diet
energy physical success
consumption obesity

Aziz Sancar Decodes the Secrets of DNA Repair

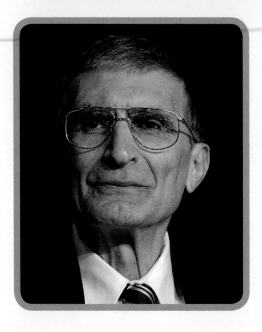

years, he worked as a doctor. Still, Sancar wanted to know more.

In 1973, Sancar immigrated to the United States. He went to graduate school in Texas. He learned about how DNA works. His research focused on repairing DNA. Sancar got his degree. He got a job in a laboratory at Yale. He kept researching. He discovered enzymes that repair DNA. They find damaged DNA and cut it out. Sancar

DNA is like an instruction book. It shows how to build human bodies. Aziz Sancar's work reveals how DNA repairs itself.

Sancar was born in 1946. His family lived in rural Turkey. His parents could not read. They wanted Sancar to be educated. Sancar liked to play soccer. But he also studied hard in school. He moved to Istanbul to study medicine. For two

100+

Number of letters Aziz Sancar received after publishing his DNA repair research.

- Sancar emigrated from Turkey in 1973 for school.
- He is a biochemist who studies how DNA works.
- He discovered how cells control DNA repair.

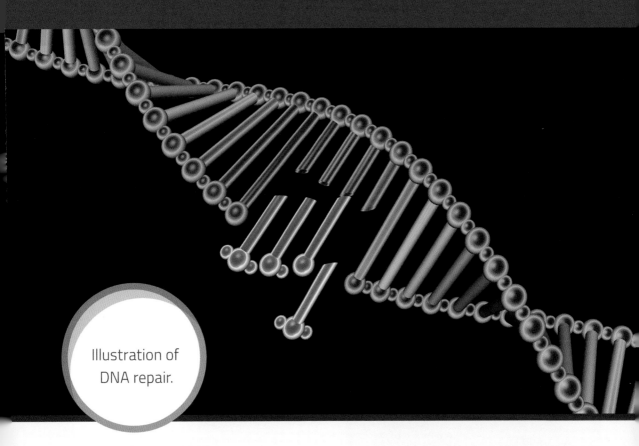

Illustration of DNA repair.

published his research. It was exciting to other scientists.

Sancar kept studying DNA repair. In 1996, he discovered something new. Every human cell has a 24-hour clock. The clock helps with DNA repair. It controls what time of day DNA is repaired. It also controls other cycles in the body, like sleep. Different times of day are better for different tasks.

Sancar's work will help develop better treatments for diseases. In 2015, he won the Nobel Prize in Chemistry.

THINK ABOUT IT

Sancar studies the clocks inside our cells. These clocks tell our bodies what time of day or night it is. What are some ways this might help our bodies work?

Inez Fung Predicts Earth's Climate Change

the storms made spirals. In school, she studied math. She thought it might help explain the spirals.

In 1967, Fung immigrated to the United States. She went to graduate school at Massachusetts Institute of Technology. There she studied math and meteorology. She liked the science of weather. She learned how hurricanes form spirals. Fung began creating mathematical models of weather.

Earth's climate is changing. Some changes can cause danger. Discovering which changes are dangerous is important. Inez Fung figured out how to test changes before they happen.

Fung was born in 1949. Her family lived on the island of Hong Kong. The ocean weather interested her. She liked to watch the clouds. Hurricanes were frightening. Fung wanted to know why

Fung worked at NASA's Goddard Institute for Space Studies. She created the first computer model of Earth's climate. In 1990, she calculated how carbon dioxide changes climate.

In 2001, Fung helped write a report. It explained how climate change works. Scientists were worried about future dangers. Fung's report was very important. Many people in the US government read it. President

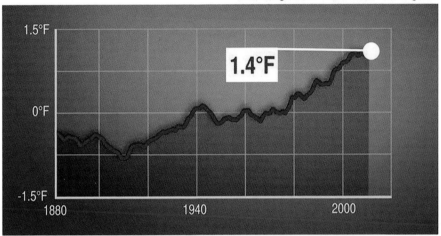

"I know a lot of really good scientists at NASA, and NOAA, and at our major universities. The best scientists in the world are all telling us that our activities are changing the climate, and if we do not act forcefully, we'll continue to see rising oceans, longer, hotter heat waves, dangerous droughts and floods, and massive disruptions that can trigger greater migration, conflict, and hunger around the globe." — President Barack Obama

WhiteHouse.gov/SOTU   #ActOnClimate   #EarthRightNow

1.4°F

NASA's analysis of the last 135 years of Earth's surface temperatures, released Jan. 16, shows a consistent, long-term warming trend: The world is now about 1.4 degrees Fahrenheit warmer than in 1880.

 EARTH *RIGHT* **NOW**

www.nasa.gov/earthrightnow

NASA's graph of the last 135 years showing Earth's long-term warming trend.

George W. Bush made a speech based on it. Climate change was a serious problem.

Today Fung works in a laboratory at the University of California, Berkeley. She is creating another model. It will predict Earth's climate changes. Scientists will use the newest information. They will test different changes. Fung's model will help plan the future.

100
Length in years of Inez Fung's climate change model predictions.

- Fung emigrated from Hong Kong in 1967 for school.
- She is a climatologist who studies how Earth's climate changes.
- Her model of Earth's climate helps predict future changes.

25

Mayly Sánchez Detects Invisible Particles

11

Number of changing neutrinos Mayly Sánchez has detected as of 2016.

- Sánchez emigrated from Venezuela in 1996 for school.
- She is a physicist who studies particles called neutrinos.
- Her research helps explain how the universe works.

The universe is old and vast. Scientists want to know more about it. Mayly Sánchez found a way to study the universe on Earth.

Sánchez was born in Venezuela in 1972. She went to school in the mountains of the Andes. She loved astronomy. She read books about the stars. Her uncle told her to study physics. It would teach her about the universe. Sánchez went to college to learn physics.

In 1996, Sánchez immigrated to the United States. She wanted a graduate degree in physics. In school, she learned about neutrinos. Neutrinos are tiny particles. They are all around us. But they are very hard to detect. Studying them reveals

Near Detector (left) and Far Detector.

NEAR AND FAR

In her research, Sánchez uses two devices called detectors. They are very large and very heavy. Both are located underground. The Near Detector is in a cavern near Chicago. The Far Detector is in northern Minnesota. It is buried 70 feet deep (21 m) in hard granite. Neutrinos zoom between the detectors at very high speeds. In less than three-millionths of a second, they travel 500 miles (805 km). The detectors record how the neutrinos change.

information about the universe. Sánchez was fascinated.

Today Sánchez works in a laboratory at Iowa State University. She develops technology to detect neutrinos. Neutrinos change as they move through space. Their changes tell her information about space. Sánchez collects the information.

In 2012, she won an award. The National Science Foundation nominated her. President Barack Obama gave her the award.

Sánchez's research is exciting. Since 2014, she has detected many neutrinos changing. She is learning new things about the universe.

More Immigrants in History

John James Audubon

Early American science owes much to a naturalist from Haiti. John James Audubon was born in 1785. At 18, he immigrated to the United States. Audubon created detailed drawings of native birds. He also studied bird migration patterns.

Cecilia Payne-Gaposchkin

In 1925, an astronomer discovered what stars are made of. Cecilia Payne was born in England in 1900. She emigrated at 23 to study at Harvard. Her theory that stars are mostly made of hydrogen was groundbreaking.

John Muir

Called America's Best Idea, the national parks were created because of John Muir. Muir was born in Scotland in 1848. His family emigrated the next year. Muir was a naturalist who convinced President Theodore Roosevelt to protect Yosemite Valley.

Severo Ochoa

The 1959 Nobel Prize in Medicine went to a Spanish American biochemist. Severo Ochoa discovered an enzyme that produces RNA in a test tube. Born in 1905 in Spain, Ochoa emigrated in 1941. His research included creating an artificial virus.

Editor's note:
America is a nation of immigrants. This series celebrates important contributions immigrants have made to science. In choosing the people to feature in this book, the author and 12 Story Library editors considered diversity of all kinds and the significance and stature of the work.

Glossary

alternating current
An electric current that reverses its direction at regular intervals.

atom
The smallest particle of material that can exist on its own.

climate
The usual weather conditions of a place over a period of years.

direct current
An electric current that flows in one direction only.

DNA
A material in the cells of plants and animals that carries genetic information.

extraterrestrial
Coming from outside Earth's atmosphere.

mass
The amount of material an object contains.

neutrino
A particle of material that is smaller than an atom and has no electrical charge.

nucleus
The central part of an atom.

ozone layer
A layer of Earth's atmosphere that blocks most of the sun's dangerous radiation from reaching Earth's surface.

radioactive
Giving off dangerous energy that is produced when atoms break apart.

relativity
A theory that says the way an object moves through space and time depends on the position and movement of someone who is watching.

theory
An idea that is intended to explain facts or events.

For More Information

Books

Berne, Jennifer, and Vladimir Radunsky. *On a Beam of Light: A Story of Albert Einstein*. San Francisco, CA: Chronicle Books, 2013.

Ignotofsky, Rachel. *Women in Science: 50 Fearless Pioneers Who Changed the World*. Berkeley, CA: Ten Speed Press, 2016.

Krull, Kathleen, and Kathryn Hewitt. *Lives of the Scientists: Experiments, Explosions (and What the Neighbors Thought)*. Boston, MA: Houghton Mifflin Harcourt, 2013.

Rusch, Elizabeth, and Oliver Dominguez. *Electrical Wizard: How Nikola Tesla Lit Up the World*. Somerville, MA: Candlewick Press, 2013.

Visit 12StoryLibrary.com

Scan the code or use your school's login at **12StoryLibrary.com** for recent updates about this topic and a full digital version of this book. Enjoy free access to:

- Digital ebook
- Breaking news updates
- Live content feeds
- Videos, interactive maps, and graphics
- Additional web resources

Note to educators: Visit 12StoryLibrary.com/register to sign up for free premium website access. Enjoy live content plus a full digital version of every 12-Story Library book you own for every student at your school.

Index

About the Author

Tristan Poehlmann is a freelance writer of educational nonfiction. He holds a master's degree in writing for children and young adults from Vermont College of Fine Arts. He lives in the San Francisco Bay Area.

READ MORE FROM 12-STORY LIBRARY

Every 12-Story Library Book is available in many fomats. For more information, visit 12StoryLibrary.com